D0049266

CLASSIC
COCKTAILS
CLASSIC & CONTEMPORARY
DRINKS TO MAKE AT HOME

CLASSIC
COCKTAILS
CLASSIC & CONTEMPORARY
DRINKS TO MAKE AT HOME

An Hachette UK Company
www.hachette.co.uk

First published in Great Britain in 2016 by Hamlyn,
an imprint of Octopus Publishing Group Ltd
Carmelite House
50 Victoria Embankment
London EC4Y 0DZ
www.octopusbooks.co.uk

This edition published in 2019 by Pyramid, an imprint of Octopus Publishing Group Ltd

ISBN 978-0-7537-3396-7

A CIP catalogue record for this book is available from the British Library

Printed and bound in China

10 9 8 7 6 5 4 3 2

For the Pyramid edition:
Publisher: Lucy Pessell
Designer: Hannah Coughlin
Editor: Sarah Vaughan
Assistant Production Manager: Lucy Carter

This material was previously published in *Drink Me Now*.

The measure that has been used in the recipes is based on a bar jigger, which is 25 ml (1 fl oz).
If preferred, a different volume can be used, providing the proportions are kept constant within
a drink and suitable adjustments are made to spoon measurements, where they occur.

Standard level spoon measurements are used in all recipes.
  1 tablespoon = one 15 ml spoon
  1 teaspoon = one 5 ml spoon

The Department of Health advises that eggs should not be consumed raw. This book contains
some recipes made with raw eggs. It is prudent for vulnerable people such as pregnant and nursing
mothers, invalids and the elderly to avoid these recipes.

This book includes recipes made with nuts and nut derivatives. It is advisable for those with
known allergic reactions to nuts and nut derivatives to avoid these recipes. It is also prudent to
check the label of pre-prepared ingredients for the possible inclusion of nut derivatives.

The UK Health Department recommends that men do not regularly exceed 3–4 units of
alcohol a day and women 2–3 units a day, a unit being defined as 10 ml of pure alcohol, the
equivalent of a single measure (25 ml) of spirits. The US Department of Health and Human
Services recommends that men do not regularly exceed 2 drinks a day and women 1 drink a
day, a drink being defined as 0.5 oz of pure alcohol, the equivalent of 1.5 oz of 80-proof distilled
spirits. Those who regularly drink more than this run an increasingly significant risk of illness and
death from a number of conditions. In addition, women who are pregnant or trying to conceive
should avoid drinking alcohol.

CONTENTS

INTRODUCTION

INGREDIENTS

Good cocktails, like good food, are based around quality ingredients. Using fresh and homemade ingredients, as with cooking, can often make a huge difference between a good drink and an outstanding drink.

ICE This is a key part of cocktails and you'll need lots of it. Purchase it from your supermarket or freeze big tubs of water, then crack this up to use in your drinks. If you're hosting a party, it may be worthwhile finding out if you have a local ice supplier, as this can be much more cost effective.

CITRUS JUICE It's important to use fresh citrus juice in your drinks; bottled versions taste awful and will not produce good drinks. Store your fruit out of the refrigerator at room temperature. Look for a soft-skinned fruit for juicing, which you can do with a juicer or citrus press. You can keep fresh citrus juice for a couple of days in the refrigerator, sealed to prevent oxidation.

SUGAR SYRUP You can buy sugar syrup to use when making cocktails or you can make your own. The key when preparing sugar syrups is to use a 1:1 ratio of sugar to liquid. You can use different types of sugar to make sugar syrup. White sugar acts as a flavour enhancer, while dark sugars have their own unique, toffee-like flavours, which work well with dark spirits.

FLAVOURED SYRUPS Again, you can buy these or make your own. There are three options for creating your own flavoured syrups.

The first option is to add a shop-bought flavoured essence to a sugar syrup made on a 1:1 ratio as described on this page. So, to make Rose Syrup, for example, add 25 ml (1 fl oz) rose essence to 1 kg (2 lb) caster sugar dissolved in 1 litre (1¾ pints) of hot water.

MAKES 1 litre (1¾ pints)

BASIC SUGAR SYRUP
**1 litre (1¾ pints) hot water
1 kg (2 lb) caster sugar**

Combine the caster sugar with the hot water and stir until the sugar has dissolved. Allow to cool.

Decant the sugar syrup into a sterilized bottle and store in the refrigerator for up to 2 weeks.

MAKES 1 litre (1¾ pints)

BASIC FLAVOURED SYRUP
**250 g (8 oz) fruit or 3 tablespoons of whole spices (not powdered)
1 litre (1¾ pints) water
1 kg (2 lb) caster sugar**

Remove any thick inedible peel from the fruit and remove any stalks, stones or pips as these will create a tannic flavour in your syrup.

Put the fruit or spices into a saucepan, add the water and bring to the boil. Reduce the heat and simmer for 30 minutes, topping up with water if required, or until the fruit is stripped of its colour. Taste the water to check how much of the flavour has leached into it.

Remove from the heat and strain into a heatproof bowl, discarding the fruit or spices. Mix the hot fruit or spice liquid with the sugar, stirring until dissolved. Allow to cool.

Decant the sugar syrup into a sterilized bottle and store in the refrigerator for up to 2 weeks.

The second option for creating a flavoured syrup is to use equal measures of strong fruit-flavoured tea and caster sugar. So, to create 1 litre (1¾ pints) of Lemon & Ginger Syrup, for example, mix 1 litre (1¾ pints) hot lemon and ginger tea with 1 kg (2 lb) caster sugar and stir until dissolved. Ensure that you remember to remove the tea bags prior to adding the sugar or things are likely to get very sticky!

The final option is to create syrups from fresh fruit, herbs or spices.

CHOOSING A GLASS

There are thousands of different cocktails, but they all fall into one of three categories: long, short or shot. Long drinks generally have more mixer than alcohol and are often served with ice and a straw. The terms 'straight up' and 'on the rocks' are synonymous with the short drink, which tends to be more about the spirit, which is often combined with a single mixer, at most. Finally, there is the shot. These miniature cocktails are made up mainly from spirits and liqueurs and are designed to give a quick hit of alcohol. Cocktail glasses are tailored to the type of drinks they will contain.

CHAMPAGNE FLUTE

Used for Champagne or Champagne cocktails, the narrow mouth of the flute helps the drink to stay fizzy.

CHAMPAGNE SAUCER

These old-fashioned glasses are not very practical for serving Champagne because the drink quickly loses its fizz.

COUPETTE OR MARGARITA GLASS

When this type of glass is used for a Margarita (see page 81), the rim is dipped in salt. These glasses are used for Daiquiris and other fruit-based cocktails.

MARTINI GLASS

A martini glass, also known as a cocktail glass, is designed so that your hand can't warm the glass, making sure that the cocktail is served completely chilled.

HIGHBALL GLASS

A highball glass is suitable for any long cocktail, from the Cuba Libre (see page 57) to Long Island Iced Tea (see page 39).

WINE GLASS

Sangria (see page 101) is often served in a wine glass, but these glasses are not usually used for cocktails.

COLLINS GLASS

This is similar to a highball glass but is slightly narrower.

OLD-FASHIONED GLASS

Also known as a rocks glass, the old-fashioned glass is great for any drink that's served on the rocks or straight up. It's also good for muddled drinks (see page 9).

SHOT GLASS

Shot glasses are often found in two sizes – for a single or double measure. They are ideal for a single mouthful, which can range from a Tequila Slammer (see page 91) to the more decadent layered B-52 (see page 125).

HURRICANE GLASS

This type of glass is mostly found in beach bars, where it is used to serve creamy rum-based drinks.

TODDY GLASS

A toddy glass is generally used for a hot drink.

SLING GLASS

This has a very short-stemmed base and is most famously used for a Singapore Sling (see page 17).

USEFUL EQUIPMENT

There are a few tools that are worth investing in if you are planning to make cocktails.

POURERS

A pourer is inserted into the top of a spirit bottle to enable the spirit to flow in a controlled manner.

MEASURE OR JIGGER

Single and double measures are available and are essential when you are mixing ingredients so that the proportions are always the same. One measure is 25 ml (1 fl oz).

HAWTHORNE STRAINER

This type of strainer is often used in conjunction with a Boston shaker, but a simple tea strainer will also work well.

MIXING GLASS

A mixing glass is used for those drinks that require only a gentle stirring before they are poured or strained.

MUDDLER

Similar to a pestle, which will work just as well, a muddler, or muddling stick, is used to crush fruit or herbs in a glass or shaker for drinks like the Mojito (see page 55).

FOOD PROCESSOR

A food processor or blender is useful for making frozen cocktails and smoothies.

BAR SPOON

Similar to a teaspoon but with a long handle, a bar spoon is used for stirring, layering and muddling drinks.

BOTTLE OPENER

Choose a bottle opener with two attachments, one for metal-topped bottles and a corkscrew for wine bottles.

COCKTAIL SHAKER

The Boston shaker is the simplest option, but it needs to be used in conjunction with a hawthorne strainer. Alternatively you could choose a shaker with a built-in strainer.

MIXOLOGY MASTERCLASS

With just a few basic techniques, your bartending skills will be complete. Follow the step-by-step instructions to hone your craft and mix perfect cocktails.

SHAKING

This is the best-known cocktail technique and probably the one that you will use most often, so it's important to get right. Shaking is used to mix ingredients quickly and thoroughly, and to chill the drink before serving.

1. Half-fill a cocktail shaker with ice cubes or cracked or crushed ice.
   If the recipe calls for a chilled glass, add a few ice cubes and some cold water to the glass, swirl it around and discard.

2. Add the recipe ingredients to the shaker and shake until a frost forms on the outside of the shaker. Use both hands, one at each end, so that it doesn't slip.
3. Strain the cocktail into the glass and serve.

BLENDING

Frozen cocktails and smoothies are blended with ice in a blender until they are of a smooth consistency. A frozen Daiquiri or Margarita is made using a virtually identical recipe to the unfrozen versions but with a scoop of crushed ice added to the blender before blending on high speed. Be careful not to add too much ice to the recipe as this will dilute the cocktail. It's best to add a little at a time.

BUILDING

This is a straightforward technique that involves nothing more than putting the ingredients together in the correct order.

1. Have all the ingredients for the cocktail to hand. Chill the glass, if required.
2. Add each ingredient in recipe order, making sure that all measures are exact.

DOUBLE-STRAINING

When you want to prevent all traces of puréed fruit and ice fragments from entering the glass, use a shaker with a built-in strainer in conjunction with a hawthorne strainer. Alternatively, strain through a fine strainer.

MUDDLING

Muddling is a technique that is used to bring out the flavours of herbs and fruit using a blunt tool called a muddler, and the best-known muddled drink is the Mojito (see page 55).

1. Add mint leaves to a highball glass, then add some sugar syrup and some lime wedges.
2. Hold the glass firmly and use a muddler or pestle to press down. Twist and press to release the flavours.
3. Continue this for about 30 seconds, then top up the glass with crushed ice and add the remaining ingredients.

LAYERING

A number of spirits can be served layered on top of each other, and because some spirits are lighter than others, they will float on top of your cocktail. One of the best-known layered drinks is the Grasshopper (see page 121).

1. Pour the first ingredient into a glass, taking care that it does not touch the sides.
2. Position a bar spoon in the centre of the glass, rounded part down and facing you. Rest the spoon against the side of the glass as you pour the second ingredient down the spoon. It should float on top of the first liquid, creating a separate layer.
3. Repeat with the third ingredient, then carefully remove the spoon.

GIN

CLASSIC MARTINI
ice cubes
I measure dry vermouth
6 measures gin
stuffed green olives, to decorate

Put 10–12 ice cubes into a mixing glass. Pour over the vermouth and gin and stir (never shake) vigorously and evenly without splashing.

Strain into 2 chilled martini glasses, decorate each with a green olive on a cocktail stick and serve.

NEGRONI
ice cubes
I measure gin
I measure sweet vermouth
I measure Campari
orange wedge, to decorate

Fill an old-fashioned glass with ice cubes, add the remaining ingredients and stir. Decorate with an orange wedge and serve.

TOM COLLINS

2 measures gin

I measure sugar syrup

I measure lemon juice

ice cubes

4 measures soda water

TO DECORATE

lemon wedge

black cherry

Pour the gin, sugar syrup and lemon juice into a cocktail shaker and fill with ice cubes.

Shake, then strain into a Collins glass full of ice cubes and top up with the soda water. Decorate with a lemon wedge and a cherry and serve.

GIN TROPICAL

8 ice cubes

I½ measures gin

I measure lemon juice

I measure passion fruit juice

½ measure orange juice

soda water, to top up

orange spiral, to decorate

Put 4 of the ice cubes into a cocktail shaker, pour in the gin and fruit juices and shake well.

Put 4 ice cubes into an old-fashioned glass and strain the cocktail over the ice. Top up with soda water and stir gently. Decorate with an orange spiral and serve.

SINGAPORE SLING

ice cubes
2 measures gin
I measure cherry brandy
½ measure Cointreau
½ measure Bénédictine
I measure grenadine
I measure lime juice
10 measures pineapple juice
1–2 dashes Angostura bitters

TO DECORATE
pineapple wedges
maraschino cherries

Half-fill a cocktail shaker with ice cubes and put some ice cubes into each highball glass. Add the remaining ingredients to the shaker and shake until a frost forms on the outside of the shaker.

Strain over the ice cubes in the glasses. Decorate each glass with a pineapple wedge and a maraschino cherry on a cocktail stick and serve.

FRENCH PINK LADY

2 measures gin
4 raspberries
I measure Triple Sec
3 teaspoons lime juice
I teaspoon pastis
ice cubes
lime wedge, to decorate

Add the gin, raspberries, Triple Sec, lime juice and pastis to a cocktail shaker and muddle. Fill the shaker with ice cubes and shake.

Strain into a martini glass, decorate with a lime wedge and serve.

BETSY

2 measures gin or vodka
4 teaspoons lime juice
1 measure sugar syrup
2 strawberries, plus extra to decorate
1 sprig coriander
1 cup ice cubes

Put all the ingredients into a food processor or blender and blend until smooth.

Pour into 2 old-fashioned glasses, decorate each with a strawberry and serve.

FRENCH 75

1 measure gin
3 teaspoons lemon juice
3 teaspoons sugar syrup
4 measures chilled Champagne
lemon twist, to decorate

Pour the gin, lemon juice and sugar syrup into a cocktail shaker and shake.

Strain into a Champagne flute and top up with the Champagne. Decorate with a lemon twist and serve.

RIVIERA FIZZ

3 measures sloe gin
I measure lemon juice
I measure sugar syrup
ice cubes
chilled Champagne, to top up
lemon twists, to decorate

Pour the sloe gin, lemon juice and sugar syrup into
a cocktail shaker and add some ice cubes.

Shake and strain into 2 chilled Champagne flutes. Top up with
Champagne, stir, decorate each glass with a lemon twist and serve.

GINNY GIN FIZZ

2 measures gin
I camomile tea bag
I measure sugar syrup
I measure lemon juice
3 teaspoons egg white
ice cubes
3 measures soda water
lemon twist, to decorate

Pour the gin into a cocktail shaker, add the tea bag and leave to infuse for 2 minutes.

Remove the tea bag and add the sugar syrup, lemon juice
and egg white. Fill the shaker with ice cubes.

Shake and strain into a wine glass filled with ice cubes and top up with the soda
water. Decorate with a lemon twist and serve.

BERRY COLLINS

8 raspberries, plus extra to decorate

8 blueberries

1–2 dashes strawberry syrup

crushed ice

4 measures gin

4 teaspoons lemon juice

sugar syrup, to taste

soda water, to top up

Put the berries and strawberry syrup into 2 highball glasses and muddle together.

Fill each glass with crushed ice. Add the gin, lemon juice and sugar syrup, stir, then top up with the soda water. Decorate each glass with raspberries and serve.

SOUTHSIDE

ice cubes

2 measures gin

4 teaspoons lime juice

4 teaspoons sugar syrup

5 mint leaves, plus extra to decorate

Add all the ingredients to a cocktail shaker. Shake and strain into a martini glass. Decorate with a mint leaf and serve.

SAPPHIRE MARTINI

ice cubes

4 measures gin

1 measure blue Curaçao

red or blue cocktail cherries, to decorate

Put 8 ice cubes into a cocktail shaker. Pour the gin and blue Curaçao over the ice and shake well to mix.

Strain into 2 martini glasses. Carefully drop a cherry into each glass and serve.

GIN CUCUMBER COOLER

2 measures gin

5 mint leaves, plus an extra sprig to decorate

5 slices cucumber

3 measures apple juice

3 measures soda water

ice cubes

Add the gin, mint and cucumber to a Collins glass and gently muddle. Leave to stand for a couple of minutes.

Add the apple juice, soda water and some ice cubes. Decorate with a sprig of mint and serve.

PINK CLOVER CLUB

ice cubes

juice of 2 limes

2 dashes grenadine

2 egg whites

6 measures gin

strawberry slices, to decorate

Put 8–10 ice cubes into a cocktail shaker. Pour the lime juice, grenadine, egg whites and gin over the ice and shake until a frost forms on the outside of the shaker.

Strain into 2 martini glasses. Decorate each glass with strawberry slices and serve.

CAMOMILE COLLINS

2 measures gin

I camomile tea bag

I measure lemon juice

I measure sugar syrup

4 measures soda water

ice cubes

lemon slice, to decorate

Pour the gin into a Collins glass and add the tea bag. Stir the tea bag and gin together until the gin is infused with camomile flavour, about 5 minutes.

Remove the tea bag and fill the glass with ice cubes. Add the remaining ingredients, decorate with a lemon slice and serve.

TANQSTREAM
cracked ice cubes
4 measures Tanqueray gin
4 teaspoons lime juice
6 measures soda water or tonic water
4 teaspoons crème de cassis

TO DECORATE
lime slices
mixed berries

Put some cracked ice cubes with the gin and lime juice into a cocktail shaker and shake to mix.

Strain into 2 highball glasses, each half-filled with cracked ice cubes. For a dry Tanqstream, add soda water; for a less dry drink, add tonic water. Stir in the crème de cassis, decorate each glass with the lime slices and mixed berries and serve.

KIWI SMASH
½ kiwi fruit, quartered, plus an extra slice to decorate
4 lemon slices
4 teaspoons sugar syrup
2 measures gin
I sprig coriander
crushed ice

Add the kiwi fruit, lemon slices and sugar syrup to an old-fashioned glass and muddle. Add the gin and coriander and half-fill the glass with crushed ice.

Churn with the muddler until thoroughly mixed. Top up with more crushed ice, decorate with a kiwi fruit slice on a cocktail stick and serve.

WATERMELON & BASIL SMASH

ice cubes

2 measures gin

3 x 1 cm (½ inch) cubes watermelon

3 basil leaves, plus extra to decorate

2 teaspoons sugar syrup

Add all the ingredients to a cocktail shaker and shake well.

Strain into a chilled martini glass. Decorate with a basil leaf floated on the surface of the liquid and serve.

GINGER RICKY

4 x 2.5 cm (1 inch) cubes pineapple

2 lime wedges

1½ measures London dry gin

½ measure ginger juice (see tip)

1 teaspoon lime juice

ice cubes

3½ measures ginger ale

pineapple wedge, to decorate

Muddle the pineapple and lime wedges in the bottom of a cocktail shaker. Add the gin and ginger and lime juices and shake well.

Strain into a highball glass filled with ice cubes and top up with the ginger ale. Decorate with a pineapple wedge and serve.

TIP: TO MAKE GINGER JUICE, PEEL A LARGE PIECE OF FRESH ROOT GINGER AND BLITZ IN A BLENDER OR FOOD PROCESSOR. STRAIN THE JUICE BEFORE USE.

VODKA

COSMOPOLITAN
ice cubes
1½ measures lemon vodka
4 teaspoons Triple Sec
3 teaspoons lime juice
I measure cranberry juice
lime slice, to decorate

Add all the ingredients to a cocktail shaker and shake.

Strain into a martini glass, decorate with a slice of lime and serve.

SEX ON THE BEACH
ice cubes
2 measures vodka
2 measures peach schnapps
2 measures cranberry juice
2 measures orange juice
2 measures pineapple juice (optional)

TO DECORATE
lemon wedges
lime wedges

Put 8–10 ice cubes into a cocktail shaker and add the vodka, schnapps, cranberry juice, orange juice and pineapple juice (if using). Shake well.

Put 3–4 ice cubes into each highball glass, strain over the cocktail and decorate each with the lemon and lime wedges.

GODMOTHER
cracked ice cubes
3 measures vodka
1 measure Amaretto di Saronno

Put 2–3 cracked ice cubes into each old-fashioned glass. Add the vodka
and Amaretto, stir lightly to mix and serve.

WHITE RUSSIAN
12 cracked ice cubes
2 measures vodka
2 measures Tia Maria
2 measures full-fat milk or double cream

Put half the cracked ice into a cocktail shaker and put the
remaining cracked ice into 2 old-fashioned glasses. Add the
vodka, Tia Maria and milk or cream to the shaker and shake
until a frost forms on the outside of the shaker.

Strain over the ice in the glasses and serve.

SEA BREEZE

ice cubes

2 measures vodka

4 measures cranberry juice

2 measures grapefruit juice

lemon rind strips, to decorate

Fill 2 highball glasses with ice cubes, pour over the vodka and fruit juices and stir well. Decorate each glass with lemon rind strips and serve.

LONG ISLAND ICED TEA

1 measure vodka

1 measure gin

1 measure white rum

1 measure tequila

1 measure Cointreau

1 measure lemon juice

ice cubes

cola, to top up

lemon slices, to decorate

Put the vodka, gin, rum, tequila, Cointreau and lemon juice in a cocktail shaker with some ice cubes and shake to mix.

Strain into 2 highball glasses filled with ice cubes and top up with cola. Decorate each glass with lemon slices and serve.

MAKES 2 * GLASSES 2 chilled martini glasses
EQUIPMENT cocktail shaker, 2 strainers, cocktail sticks

VALENTINE MARTINI

ice cubes
4 measures raspberry vodka
12 raspberries, plus extra to decorate
1 measure lime juice
2 dashes sugar syrup
lime spirals, to decorate

Half-fill a cocktail shaker with ice cubes. Add all the remaining ingredients and shake until a frost forms on the outside of the shaker.

Double-strain into 2 chilled martini glasses. Decorate each glass with raspberries and lime spirals on cocktail sticks and serve.

MAKES 1 * GLASSES 1 old-fashioned glass
EQUIPMENT cocktail shaker, muddler, strainer

PINK COOLER

5 watermelon chunks, plus extra to decorate
2 measures lemon vodka
ice cubes
2 measures bitter lemon

Muddle the watermelon in the bottom of a cocktail shaker. Add the vodka and shake.

Strain into an old-fashioned glass full of ice cubes and top up with the bitter lemon. Decorate with a chunk of watermelon and serve.

RISING SUN

ice cubes
4 measures vodka
4 teaspoons passion fruit syrup
6 measures grapefruit juice
pink grapefruit slices, to decorate

Half-fill a cocktail shaker with ice cubes and put 6–8 ice cubes into each old-fashioned glass.

Add all the remaining ingredients to the shaker and shake until a frost forms on the outside of the shaker.

Strain into the glasses, decorate each with a pink grapefruit slice and serve.

VODKA SAZERAC

2 sugar cubes
4 drops Angostura bitters
5 drops Pernod
6–8 ice cubes
4 measures vodka
lemonade, to top up

Put the sugar cubes in 2 old-fashioned glasses and shake the bitters on top.

Add the Pernod and swirl it around to coat the inside of each glass.

Drop in the ice cubes and pour in the vodka. Top up with lemonade, stir gently to mix and serve.

LONG BLUSH

I measure vodka

2 teaspoons clear honey

I measure pomegranate juice

2 teaspoons lime juice

I measure rosé wine

5 mint leaves

2 measures soda water

crushed ice

TO DECORATE

mint sprig

pomegranate seeds

Add the vodka, honey, pomegranate and lime juices, wine and mint leaves to a cocktail shaker and shake.

Strain into a sling glass and add the soda water. Top up the glass with crushed ice, decorate with a mint sprig and some pomegranate seeds and serve.

LYCHEE MARTINI

ice cubes

2 measures vodka

3 lychees, plus extra to decorate

I measure Triple Sec

3 teaspoons lemon juice

Add all the ingredients to a cocktail shaker and muddle.

Shake, then strain into a martini glass. Decorate with a lychee on a cocktail stick and serve.

BUCK'S TWIZZ

2 measures chilled orange juice
I measure maraschino liqueur
2 measures Absolut Mandarin vodka
chilled Champagne, to top up
rindless pink grapefruit slices, to decorate

Pour the orange juice and maraschino into 2 chilled
Champagne saucers.

Add the vodka and Champagne at the same time
(this prevents excessive fizzing). Decorate each glass
with a rindless pink grapefruit slice and serve.

RUSSIAN SPRING PUNCH

ice cubes
I measure crème de cassis
2 measures lemon juice
4 tablespoons sugar syrup
chilled Champagne, to top up
4 measures Absolut vodka

TO DECORATE
lemon slices
mixed berries

Fill 2 highball glasses with ice cubes. Pour the crème de
cassis, lemon juice and sugar syrup over the ice.

Add the Champagne and vodka at the same time
(this prevents excessive fizzing) and stir. Decorate each
glass with a lemon slice and some berries and serve.

MINT ZING TING

2 lime wedges

4 mint leaves

2 dashes sugar syrup

2 measures apple-flavoured vodka

ice cubes

cucumber strips, to decorate

Muddle the lime wedges, mint and sugar syrup in the bottom of a cocktail shaker, then add the vodka and some ice cubes. Shake briefly.

Strain into 2 chilled shot glasses, decorate each with a cucumber strip and serve.

DAWA

2 limes, quartered and thickly sliced

2 tablespoons thick honey

2 teaspoons caster sugar

crushed ice

4 measures vodka

Put the lime slices, honey and sugar in 2 old-fashioned glasses and muddle together.

Add some crushed ice, pour the vodka over the ice and serve.

WATERMELON PUNCH

1 watermelon (about 9 kg/20 lb)
200 ml (7 fl oz) vodka
20 mint leaves
3 measures lemon juice
5 measures sugar syrup
1 cup ice cubes
lemon slice, to decorate

Cut the top off the watermelon and use a spoon to scoop out
the flesh inside. Set aside the hollowed-out watermelon.

Remove the pips from the watermelon flesh, then add the flesh and
the remaining ingredients to a food processor or blender
and blend until smooth.

Pour into the hollowed-out watermelon, decorate with a lemon slice
and serve with straws.

MAKES 2 ✳ GLASSES 2 shot glasses ✳ EQUIPMENT cocktail shaker, strainer

LEMON DROP

ice cubes
1½ measures lemon vodka
1½ measures limoncello
1 dash lemon juice
1 dash lime cordial

Put some ice cubes into a cocktail shaker, add the vodka,
limoncello, lemon juice and lime cordial and shake briefly.

Strain into 2 shot glasses and serve.

RUM

DAIQUIRI

ice cubes
2 measures light rum
1 measure sugar syrup
1 measure lime juice
lime wedge, to decorate

Add all the ingredients to a cocktail shaker and shake.

Strain into a martini glass, decorate with a lime wedge and serve.

MOJITO

16 mint leaves, plus sprigs to decorate
1 lime, cut into wedges
4 teaspoons cane sugar
crushed ice
5 measures white rum
soda water, to top up

Muddle the mint leaves, lime and sugar in the bottom
of 2 highball glasses and fill with crushed ice.

Add the rum, stir and top up with soda water.
Decorate each glass with mint sprigs and serve.

CUBA LIBRE

ice cubes
2 measures golden rum, such as Havana Club 3-year-old
juice of ½ lime
cola, to top up
lime wedges, to decorate

Fill an old-fashioned or highball glass with ice cubes. Pour over the rum and lime juice and stir.

Top up with cola, decorate with lime wedges and serve with a straw.

GOLDEN APRICOT

3 tablespoons rum
3 teaspoons apricot liqueur
4 teaspoons lime juice
4 teaspoons sugar syrup
I egg yolk
ice cubes
4 measures soda water
dried apricot, to decorate

Put the rum, apricot liqueur, lime juice, sugar syrup and egg yolk into a food processor or blender and blend.

Strain into a Collins glass and fill the glass with ice cubes before topping up with the soda water. Decorate with a dried apricot on a cocktail stick and serve with a straw.

RUM OLD-FASHIONED

6 ice cubes

2 dashes Angostura bitters

2 dashes lime bitters

2 teaspoons caster sugar

1 measure water

4 measures white rum

1 measure dark rum

lime twists, to decorate

Put 2 ice cubes, both bitters, the sugar and water into 2 old-fashioned glasses and stir until the sugar has dissolved.

Add the white rum, stir and add the remaining ice cubes. Add the dark rum and stir again. Decorate each glass with a lime twist and serve.

MAKES 2 * GLASSES 2 hurricane glasses * EQUIPMENT food processor, straws

TIKI TREAT

crushed ice

1 ripe mango, peeled and stoned, plus extra slices to decorate

6 coconut chunks

2 measures coconut cream

4 measures aged rum

2 dashes lemon juice

2 teaspoons caster sugar

Put a small scoop of crushed ice with all the other ingredients into a food processor or blender and blend until smooth.

Pour into 2 hurricane glasses, decorate each glass with mango slices and serve with straws.

SPICED BERRY

ice cubes
2 measures Captain Morgan Spiced Rum
2 dashes lime juice
2 dashes raspberry purée
2 dashes sugar syrup
raspberries, to decorate

Put some ice cubes into a cocktail shaker, pour the rum, lime juice,
raspberry purée and sugar syrup over the ice and shake briefly.

Strain into 2 chilled shot glasses, decorate each glass
with a raspberry and serve.

GOOMBAY SMASH

3 measures coconut rum
2 measures cachaça
I measure apricot brandy
I measure lime juice
8 measures pineapple juice
ice cubes

TO DECORATE
pineapple wedges
lime twists
maraschino cherries

Put the rum, cachaça, brandy and fruit juices in a cocktail
shaker and add some ice cubes.

Shake and strain over more ice into 2 old-fashioned
glasses. Decorate each glass with a pineapple wedge, a lime
twist and some cherries on cocktail sticks and serve.

ST CLEMENTS COLLINS

1½ measures white rum

1 citrus tea bag

ice cubes

2 teaspoons lemon juice

1 teaspoon caster sugar

soda water, to top up

orange or lemon twist, to decorate

Pour the rum into a wine glass, add the tea bag and leave
to steep for 2 minutes.

Remove the tea bag and add some ice cubes to the glass. Add the
remaining ingredients and stir. Decorate with a twist of orange or
lemon and serve.

DUKE'S DAIQUIRI

2 measures white rum

3 teaspoons lime juice

1 measure sugar syrup

tinned peach half, drained

1 measure cloudy apple juice

1 teaspoon grenadine

1 cup ice cubes

TO DECORATE

lime slice

black cherry

Add all ingredients to a food processor or blender and
blend until smooth.

Pour into a hurricane glass, decorate with a lime slice
and a cherry and serve.

CAPRISSIMA DA UVA

½ lime, plus a lime slice to decorate

5 red grapes, plus extra to decorate

2 measures amber rum

2 teaspoons caster sugar

2 teaspoons velvet falernum

crushed ice

Muddle the lime and grapes at the bottom of an old-fashioned glass. Add the rum, sugar and velvet falernum and half-fill the glass with crushed ice.

Churn the mixture with a muddler until thoroughly mixed. Top the glass up with more crushed ice, decorate with a lime slice and grape and serve.

HOPPER'S FIX

1½ measures dark rum

1 measure espresso (cooled to room temperature or chilled)

½ teaspoon chocolate hazelnut spread

ice cubes

3 coffee beans, to decorate

Put the rum, espresso and chocolate hazelnut spread into a cocktail shaker. Muddle the ingredients well in order to dissolve the chocolate hazelnut chocolate spread. Add several ice cubes and shake well until a frost forms on the outside of the shaker.

Strain into a martini glass. Decorate with the coffee beans floated in a cluster on the surface and serve.

WHISKY

OLD-FASHIONED

ice cubes

2 measures bourbon

1 teaspoon sugar syrup

1 dash orange bitters

1 dash Angostura bitters

orange twist, to decorate

Half-fill an old-fashioned glass with ice cubes. Add the remaining ingredients to the glass and stir for 1 minute.

Fill the glass with more ice cubes. Decorate with an orange twist and serve.

WHISKY HIGHBALL

ice cubes

2 measures Scotch whisky

1 dash Angostura bitters

4 measures soda water

lemon twist, to decorate

Add 3 large ice cubes and the whisky and bitters to a highball glass.

Stir gently, then fill the glass with more ice cubes and top up with the soda water. Decorate with a lemon twist and serve.

WILLIAM'S PEAR

½ ripe pear, cut into chunks, plus pear slices to decorate

3 teaspoons redcurrant jam

2 measures bourbon

4 teaspoons lemon juice

2 teaspoons sugar syrup

ice cubes

Muddle the pear and jam in the bottom of a cocktail shaker. Add the
remaining ingredients and shake.

Strain into an old-fashioned glass full of ice cubes,
decorate with pear slices and serve.

GINGER FIX

ice cubes

I measure blended Scotch whisky

I measure ginger wine

2 dashes Angostura bitters

4 measures soda water

lemon wedge, to decorate

Fill the Collins glass with ice cubes, add the remaining
ingredients and stir. Decorate with a lemon wedge
and serve.

STONE FENCE

1 crisp apple, plus an apple slice, to decorate
ice cubes
2 measures rye whiskey
1 measure soda water

Juice the apple and pour the juice into an old-fashioned glass full of ice cubes.

Add the whiskey and soda water. Decorate with an apple slice and serve.

RUSTY NAIL

ice cubes
3 measures Scotch whisky
2 measures Drambuie

Fill 2 old-fashioned glasses with ice cubes. Pour the whisky and Drambuie over the ice and serve.

WHISKY SOUR

ice cubes
2 measures Scotch whisky
I measure lemon juice
I measure sugar syrup

TO DECORATE
lemon wedge
lemon spirals

Fill a cocktail shaker with ice cubes. Add the remaining
ingredients and shake.

Strain into an old-fashioned glass filled with ice cubes, decorate with a
lemon wedge and a lemon spiral and serve.

PINEAPPLE JULEP

I½ measures bourbon
10 mint leaves
2 teaspoons cardamom syrup (see tip)
2 measures pineapple juice
crushed ice
pineapple leaves, to decorate

Add the bourbon, mint leaves, cardamom syrup and
pineapple juice to a julep tin or jam jar and churn together
with a muddler.

Fill the tin or jam jar with crushed ice, decorate with
pineapple leaves and serve with a straw.

TIP: TO MAKE THE CARDAMOM SYRUP, STEEP
20 CARDAMOM PODS IN 500 ML (17 FL OZ) SUGAR
SYRUP FOR 48 HOURS, AND STRAIN.

SCOTCH GINGER HIGHBALL

ice cubes

2 measures Scotch whisky

I measure lemon juice

3 teaspoons sugar syrup

4 measures ginger ale

mint sprigs, to decorate

Pour the whisky, lemon juice, sugar syrup and ginger ale into a highball glass filled with ice cubes and stir. Decorate with mint sprigs and serve.

MAKES 2 * GLASSES 2 old-fashioned glasses * EQUIPMENT cocktail shaker, strainer

ZOOM

ice cubes

4 measures Scotch whisky

2 teaspoons clear honey

2 measures chilled water

2 measures single cream

Put 8–10 ice cubes into a cocktail shaker, add the whisky, honey, chilled water and cream and shake well.

Strain into 2 old-fashioned glasses and serve at once.

TEQUILA

MARGARITA

2 lime wedges
rock salt
4 measures Herradura Reposado tequila
2 measures lime juice
2 measures Triple Sec
ice cubes
lime slices, to decorate

Dampen the rim of each coupette or margarita glass with a lime
wedge, then dip it into a saucer of rock salt.

Pour the tequila, lime juice and Triple Sec into a cocktail shaker, add
some ice cubes and shake.

Strain into the prepared glasses, decorate each with a slice
of lime and serve.

FRESH PALOMA

½ pink grapefruit, peeled
ice cubes
2 measures blanco tequila
2 measures soda water
1 teaspoon agave syrup
pink grapefruit wedge, to decorate

Juice the pink grapefruit and pour the juice into a Collins
glass full of ice cubes.

Add the remaining ingredients, decorate with a grapefruit
wedge and serve.

COCONUT & LIME MARGARITA

ice cubes

3 measures 100 per cent agave tequila

4 teaspoons lime cordial

4 teaspoons coconut syrup

3 measures pineapple juice

1 measure lime juice

lime slices, to decorate

Combine the ingredients in a cocktail shaker and shake well until
a frost forms on the outside of the shaker.

Strain into 2 martini glasses and decorate each with a lime slice.

WATERMELON SMASH

1 measure tequila

4 watermelon chunks

5 mint leaves, plus an extra sprig to decorate

1 teaspoon agave syrup

1 cup crushed ice

Add all the ingredients to a food processor or blender
and blend until smooth.

Pour into an old-fashioned glass, decorate with a mint
sprig and serve.

LOS ALTOS

5 slices tangerine

3 teaspoons agave syrup

2 measures tequila

2 teaspoons lime juice

2 teaspoons Campari

ice cubes

4 measures soda water

TO DECORATE

orange slice

lime slice

Add the tangerine slices and agave syrup to a cocktail shaker and muddle. Pour in the tequila, lime juice and Campari and shake.

Strain into a Collins glass filled with ice cubes and top up with the soda water. Decorate with an orange slice and a lime slice and serve.

SILK STOCKING

drinking chocolate powder

1½ measures tequila

1½ measures white crème de cacao

7 measures single cream

4 teaspoons grenadine

ice cubes

Dampen the rim of 2 chilled martini glasses and dip them into a saucer of drinking chocolate powder.

Pour the tequila, crème de cacao, cream and grenadine into a cocktail shaker and add 8–10 ice cubes. Shake vigorously for 10 seconds, then strain into the prepared glasses and serve.

JALISCO

crushed ice
1½ measures tequila
10 cm (4 inch) piece cucumber
1 coriander sprig
2 teaspoons lime juice
4 pineapple wedges
1 teaspoon agave syrup
ice cubes

TO DECORATE
twist of black pepper
cucumber slice

Add all ingredients to a food processor or blender with some ice cubes and blend until well combined.

Pour into a Collins glass, top with black pepper and a cucumber slice and serve.

BAJA SOUR

ice cubes
2½ measures tequila gold
4 teaspoons sugar syrup
2½ measures lemon juice
4 dashes orange bitters
1 egg white
2 tablespoons amontillado sherry

TO DECORATE
lemon wedges
orange spirals

Put 8–10 ice cubes into a cocktail shaker with the tequila, sugar syrup, lemon juice, bitters and egg white and shake vigorously.

Pour into 2 highball glasses and drizzle over the sherry. Decorate each glass with a lemon wedge and an orange spiral and serve.

SOUTH FOR THE SUMMER

4 teaspoons grenadine

4 measures tequila

6 measures orange juice

8 fresh pineapple chunks

crushed ice

TO DECORATE

pineapple leaves

orange spirals

Pour the grenadine gently into 2 highball glasses.

Put the tequila, orange juice and pineapple chunks into a food processor or blender with some crushed ice and blend until slushy.

Pour the mixture over the grenadine. Decorate each glass with a pineapple leaf and an orange spiral and stir just before serving.

MAKES 2 ✳ GLASSES 2 highball glasses

MEXICAN BULLDOG

ice cubes

1½ measures tequila

1½ measures Kahlúa coffee liqueur

2½ measures single cream

7 measures cola

drinking chocolate powder, to decorate

Put 4–6 ice cubes in 2 highball glasses. Pour in the tequila, Kahlúa and cream, then top up with the cola.

Stir gently, sprinkle with drinking chocolate powder and serve.

TIJUANA MARY

4 watermelon chunks, plus a watermelon wedge to decorate

2 measures tequila

2 teaspoons sriracha sauce

I pinch salt

2 pinches pink peppercorns

ice cubes

4 measures tomato juice

Place the watermelon chunks in a cocktail shaker and muddle. Add the tequila, sriracha sauce, salt, peppercorns and some ice cubes and shake.

Strain into a Collins glass full of ice cubes and top up with the tomato juice. Stir well, decorate with a watermelon wedge and serve.

TEQUILA SLAMMER

2 measures tequila gold

2 measures chilled Champagne

Pour the tequila into 2 shot glasses. Slowly top up with the Champagne.

Cover the top of the glass with the palm of your hand to seal the contents inside and grip it with your fingers. Briskly pick up the glass and slam it down on a surface to make the drink fizz. Quickly gulp it down in one, while it's still fizzing.

BRANDY & SHERRY

BRANDY CRUSTA

lemon wedges

caster sugar

4 measures brandy

I measure orange Curaçao

I measure maraschino liqueur

2 measures lemon juice

6 dashes Angostura bitters

ice cubes

lemon rind strips, to decorate

Dampen the rim of each chilled martini glass with a lemon wedge, then dip into a saucer of caster sugar.

Put the brandy, Curaçao, maraschino, lemon juice and bitters into a cocktail shaker with some ice cubes and shake well.

Strain into the prepared glasses, decorate each with lemon rind strips and serve.

ABC COCKTAIL

ice cubes

I measure VSOP Cognac

I measure tawny port

2 teaspoons maraschino liqueur

6 mint leaves, plus extra to decorate

Add all the ingredients to a cocktail shaker and shake.

Strain into a martini glass, decorate with a mint leaf and serve.

MONTE CARLO SLING

10 grapes, plus extra to decorate

crushed ice

2 measures brandy

1 measure peach liqueur

2 measures ruby port

2 measures lemon juice

1 measure orange juice

2 dashes orange bitters

4 measures chilled Champagne

Muddle 5 grapes in the bottom of each highball glass, then
fill each glass with crushed ice.

Put all the other ingredients, except the Champagne, into
a cocktail shaker and add more ice. Shake well.

Strain into the glasses and top up with the Champagne. Decorate each
glass with grapes on cocktail sticks and serve.

JACK ROSE

ice cubes

2 measures apple brandy

3 teaspoons grenadine

4 teaspoons lemon juice

Add all the ingredients to a cocktail shaker. Shake, strain
into a martini glass and serve.

PUDDING COCKTAIL

2 measures Calvados

3 measures brandy

2 egg yolks

2 teaspoons caster sugar

ice cubes

ground cinnamon, to decorate

Put the Calvados, brandy, egg yolks and caster sugar into a cocktail shaker with some ice cubes and shake until well mixed.

Strain into 2 chilled martini glasses. Light a long taper, hold it over each glass in turn and sprinkle cinnamon through the flame on to the surface of the drink. Serve at once.

JAFFA

ice cubes

2 measures brandy

2 measures dark crème de cacao

2 measures single cream

1 measure Mandarine Napoléon

4 dashes orange bitters

orange-flavoured chocolate shavings, to decorate

Half-fill a cocktail shaker with ice cubes. Add the remaining ingredients and shake until a frost forms on the outside of the shaker.

Strain into 2 chilled martini glasses, decorate with orange-flavoured chocolate shavings and serve.

VALENCIAN SANGRIA

ice cubes

I measure brandy

2 measures blood orange juice

I pinch pink peppercorns

I measure sweet vermouth

2 teaspoons Campari

2 measures red wine

2 measures soda water

orange slice, to decorate

Fill a wine glass with ice cubes. Add all the remaining ingredients and stir.

Decorate with an orange slice and serve.

MAKES I ∗ GLASSES I wine glass ∗ EQUIPMENT cocktail shaker, muddler, strainer

PISCO PUNCH

2 measures pisco

2 pineapple chunks

I measure orange juice

4 teaspoons lime juice

2 teaspoons velvet falernum

2 teaspoons sugar syrup

2 dashes Angostura bitters

ice cubes

pineapple wedge, to decorate

Add all the ingredients to a cocktail shaker and muddle.

Shake, then strain into a wine glass filled with ice cubes. Decorate with a pineapple wedge and serve.

SHERRY PUNCH

5 pineapple chunks

5 raspberries

3 lemon slices

2 teaspoons sugar syrup

2 measures fino sherry

crushed ice

TO DECORATE

pineapple wedge

raspberry

Add the pineapple chunks, raspberries, lemon slices and sugar syrup to a cocktail shaker and muddle. Add the sherry and shake.

Strain into an old-fashioned glass full of crushed ice, decorate with a pineapple wedge and a raspberry on a cocktail stick and serve.

FIFTH AVENUE

2 measures crème de cacao

2 measures apricot brandy

2 measures single cream

Pour the crème de cacao into 2 straight-sided shot glasses. Using the back of a bar spoon, slowly float the apricot brandy over the crème de cacao to form a separate layer.

Layer the cream over the apricot brandy in the same way and serve.

CHAMPAGNE, PROSECCO & WINE

MANDARIN 75

3 teaspoons mandarin oleo-saccharum (see tip)
I measure chilled orange juice
4 measures chilled Champagne
orange twist, to decorate

Add the oleo-saccharum to a Champagne flute, pour in the orange juice and Champagne and stir gently. Decorate with an orange twist on a cocktail stick and serve.

TIP: OLEO-SACCHARUM IS A SYRUP PRODUCED FROM THE OIL OF CITRUS RIND AND SUGAR. TO MAKE MANDARIN OLEO-SACCHARUM, WASH I MANDARIN, THEN USE A VEGETABLE PEELER TO PEEL THE RIND FROM THE FRUIT, REMOVING AS LITTLE WHITE PITH AS POSSIBLE. PLACE THE RIND IN A SMALL BOWL, ADD 3 TABLESPOONS CASTER SUGAR AND PRESS THE SUGAR AND RIND FIRMLY WITH A MUDDLER UNTIL THE RIND BEGINS TO EXPRESS OILS. ALLOW THE MIXTURE TO SIT AT ROOM TEMPERATURE FOR AN HOUR UNTIL THE SUGAR HAS DISSOLVED.

PRIMROSE FIZZ

4 mint leaves
ice cubes
4 teaspoons elderflower liqueur
I measure apple juice
4 measures chilled Champagne
apple slice, to decorate

Bruise the mint leaves and then place them in a small wine glass.

Fill the glass with ice cubes, add the remaining ingredients and stir. Decorate with an apple slice and serve.

BELLINI

½ ripe white peach
2 teaspoons sugar syrup
5 measures chilled Prosecco

Put the peach and sugar syrup into a food processor or blender and blend until smooth.

Strain into a Champagne flute, top with the Prosecco and serve.

COBBLER FIZZ

3 slices mandarin
2 raspberries, plus extra to decorate
2 teaspoons sugar syrup
1 measure fino sherry
4 measures chilled Prosecco

Add the mandarin, raspberries and sugar syrup to a cocktail shaker and muddle. Add the sherry and shake.

Strain into a Champagne flute and top up with the Prosecco. Decorate with a raspberry on a cocktail stick and serve.

RITZ FIZZ

2 dashes blue Curaçao
2 dashes lemon juice
2 dashes Amaretto di Saronno
chilled Champagne, to top up
lemon spirals, to decorate

Pour the Curaçao, lemon juice and Amaretto into a mixing glass and mix together.

Transfer to 2 Champagne flutes and top up with Champagne. Stir gently to mix, decorate each glass with a lemon spiral and serve.

ROSSINI

4 strawberries
2 teaspoons sugar syrup
5 measures chilled Prosecco

Put the strawberries and sugar syrup into a food processor or blender and blend until smooth.

Strain into a Champagne flute, top up with the Prosecco and serve.

GLÖGG

2 bottles dry red wine or 1 bottle red wine and 1 bottle port or Madeira	20 whole cloves
	175 g (6 oz) blanched almonds
rind of 1 orange	250 g (8 oz) raisins
20 cardamom pods, lightly crushed	250–375 g (8–12 oz) sugar cubes
2 cinnamon sticks	300 ml (½ pint) Aquavit or brandy

Put the wine or wine and port or Madeira into a saucepan.
Tie the orange rind and spices in a piece of muslin and add
to the pan. Add the almonds and raisins. Heat at just below
boiling point for 25 minutes, stirring occasionally.

Put a wire rack over the pan and put the sugar cubes on
it. Warm the Aquavit or brandy and pour it over the sugar
cubes to saturate them evenly. Set them alight: they will
melt through the wire rack into the wine.

Stir the Glögg and remove the spice bag. Serve hot, putting
a few raisins and almonds in each cup.

COTTER KIR

ice cubes

2 teaspoons crème de cassis

2 teaspoons crème de framboise

1 measure cranberry juice

3 measures rosé wine

3 measures soda water

raspberries, to decorate

Fill a wine glass with ice cubes. Add the remaining
ingredients and stir. Decorate with a couple of raspberries
on a cocktail stick and serve.

CLOUDY COOLER

5 white grapes, plus I extra, halved, to decorate

4 measures white wine

2 measures cloudy apple juice

I teaspoon passion fruit syrup

ice cubes

2 measures soda water

pear slice, to decorate

Muddle the grapes in the bottom of a cocktail shaker. Add the wine, apple juice and passion fruit syrup and shake.

Strain into a highball glass full of ice cubes and top up with soda water. Decorate with a pear slice and a grape, halved, on a cocktail stick and serve.

PINK SANGRIA

3 measures rosé wine

2 teaspoons agave syrup

ice cubes

2 measures pomegranate juice

2 measures lemon verbena tea

2 measures soda water

pink grapefruit slice, to decorate

Pour the wine into a wine glass, add I teaspoon of the agave syrup and stir until it dissolves.

Fill the glass up with ice cubes and add the remaining agave syrup, the pomegranate juice, lemon verbena tea and soda water. Decorate with a slice of pink grapefruit and serve.

OTHER

SPIRITS &

LIQUEURS

BITTER SPRING

ice cubes
1 measure Aperol
2 measures grapefruit juice
4 measures soda water
grapefruit wedge, to decorate

Pour the Aperol, grapefruit juice and soda water into an old-fashioned glass full of ice cubes and stir. Decorate with a grapefruit wedge and serve.

PIMM'S CUCUMBER RANGOON

ice cubes
2 measures Pimm's No. 1 Cup
2 measures cucumber juice (see tip)
3½ measures ginger ale

TO DECORATE
cucumber strips
orange slices
blueberries

Pour all the ingredients into a Collins glass filled with ice cubes. Stir well, decorate with cucumber strips twisted around the edgeof the glass, orange slices and blueberries, and serve with a straw.

TIP: TO MAKE CUCUMBER JUICE, PEEL A CUCUMBER AND THEN PROCESS IT IN A BLENDER OR JUICER. STRAIN THE JUICE BEFORE USE.

BATIDA MARACUJA

4 measures cachaça
4 passion fruit, cut in half and the pulp squeezed out
2 measures sugar syrup
2 measures lemon juice
ice cubes, plus crushed ice to serve

Put the cachaça, passion fruit pulp, sugar syrup and lemon juice into a cocktail shaker and add some ice cubes.

Shake and strain into 2 highball glasses filled with crushed ice and serve with straws.

GRASSHOPPER

2 measures white crème de cacao
2 measures crème de menthe
mint sprigs, to decorate

Pour the crème de cacao into 2 martini glasses.

Using the back of a bar spoon, slowly float the crème de menthe over the crème de cacao to form a separate layer. Decorate each glass with mint sprigs and serve.

E = MC²

crushed ice
4 measures Southern Comfort
2 measures lemon juice
1 measure maple syrup
chilled Champagne, to top up
lemon rind strips, to decorate

Put some crushed ice into a cocktail shaker. Pour the Southern Comfort, lemon juice and maple syrup over the ice and shake until a frost forms on the outside of the shaker.

Strain into 2 Champagne flutes and top up with Champagne. Decorate each glass with a lemon rind strip and serve.

FLAMING LAMBORGHINI

2 measures Kahlúa coffee liqueur
2 measures Sambuca
2 measures Bailey's Irish Cream
2 measures blue Curaçao

Pour the Kahlúa into 2 warmed martini glasses. Using the back of a bar spoon, slowly float half a measure of Sambuca over the Kahlúa to form a separate layer.

Pour the Bailey's and Curaçao into shot glasses.

Next, pour the remaining Sambuca into a warmed wine glass and carefully set it alight. Carefully pour it into the martini glasses.

Pour the Bailey's and Curaçao into the lighted martini glasses at the same time. Serve with straws.

COWGIRL
2 measures chilled peach schnapps
1 measure Bailey's Irish Cream
peach wedges

Pour the schnapps into 2 shot glasses, then, using the back of a bar spoon, slowly float the Bailey's over the schnapps to form a separate layer.

Place a peach wedge on the rim of each glass – to be eaten after the shot has been drunk – and serve.

B-52
1 measure Kahlúa coffee liqueur
1 measure Bailey's Irish Cream
1 measure Grand Marnier

Pour the Kahlúa into 2 shot glasses. Using the back of a bar spoon, slowly float the Bailey's over the Kahlúa to form a separate layer.

Layer the Grand Marnier over the Bailey's in the same way and serve.

INDEX

PICTURE CREDITS